First published in this format 2014

Text and Projects: Cathie Filian & Steve Piacenza
Cover and Interior Design: Kimberly Adis
Photographer: Alexandra Grablewski
Executive Editor, Series: Shawna Mullen
Assistant Editor, Series: Timothy Stobierski
Series Art Director: Rosalind Loeb Wanke
Series Production Editor: Lynne Phillips
Copy Editor: Candace B. Levy

The Taunton Press
Inspiration for hands-on living®

The Taunton Press, Inc., 63 South Main Street,
PO Box 5506, Newtown, CT 06470-5506
e-mail: tp@taunton.com

Threads® is a trademark of The Taunton Press, Inc.,
registered in the U.S. Patent and Trademark Office.

The following names/manufacturers appearing in
DecoDen Desserts are trademarks: Amazon®, E6000®,
eBay®, Etsy™, FIMO®, Michaels®, Mod Podge®, Sculpy®,
Styrofoam®

Library of Congress Cataloging-in-Publication Data in
progress

ISBN: 978-1-62710-970-3

Printed in the United States of America
10 9 8 7 6 5 4 3 2 1

contents

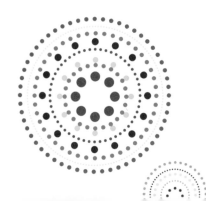

what is DecoDen?

DecoDen is the art of decorating objects in an over-the-top design.
Hailing from Japan, this craft craze screams all things cute, glitzy, and sweet. The roots of DecoDen crafts came from the art of decorating cell phone cases. Since its sparkly beginning, it has spread into decorating everything from furniture and pocket mirrors to jewelry and sneakers.

A common embellishing theme in DecoDen is decorating with cookies, cakes, and candy. One can find these sweet treats embellishing almost any style of DecoDen craft. Some embellishments are miniature versions of real sweets that look good enough to eat, and others are fantasy versions that look like they are straight from a pop music video. Both versions are equally cute and no calorie.

The whip used in DecoDen crafts resembles cake icing, and the dimensional fabric paint (aka drizzle) resembles drippy dessert sauces like chocolate and strawberry sauce. These two media are perfect for crafters who want to take the next step in DecoDen and make actual faux treats and desserts. Faux sweets that look good enough to eat can be made to scale or in miniature. They are fun to do and make the perfect gifts for friends or decorations for the house. A miniature set is perfect for a child's tea table or play kitchen.

DecoDen is all about fun and whimsy. The moment when you think you can't add one more rhinestone to a design is the exact moment when you should. A little more bling can't hurt. Here you will find all the instructions to get you started on no-bake glammed-up desserts, cakes, and parfaits, along with DecoDen classics like cellphone cases, jewelry, and everything in between. DecoDen is a craft for all, it's easy to do, and the results are fun. So grab some whip and mini sweets and start decorating!

tools

PIPING BAG AND TIPS

These are perfect to use with your whip. You can either dispense whip into a piping bag or simply (but securely) tape a piping tip over the nozzle of a squeeze tube.

TWEEZERS OR WAX PENCIL

Either of these are perfect for picking up and placing tiny rhinestones on your projects.

SANDPAPER

Sandpaper is great for roughing up the surface of your project a bit before you begin gluing on your materials—removing the slickness that you often find on phone cases and other items will allow the adhesives and embellishments to attach more securely.

PLASTIC ORGANIZER

Perfect for organizing your cabochons, rhinestones, and other embellishments.

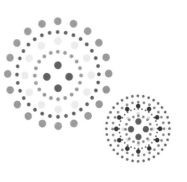

embellishments

CABOCHONS

A cabochon typically refers to a stone that has been polished as opposed to faceted. Cabochons historically have a convex form with a flat back. The flat back is the important aspect of cabochons used in DecoDen, as it allows them to attach unobtrusively to an object. Cabochons can be purchased from various websites (see Resources on p. 30) or made using silicone molds with resin, using polymer clay, or melting colored sticks with a glue gun. See "Make Your Own Cabochons" below for tips.

RHINESTONES

Rhinestones add bling to any DecoDen project and come in both large and small varieties. Use them sparingly or in excess to add sparkle and whimsy to your project.

FLAT-BACK PLASTIC PEARLS

Pearls work similarly to rhinestones, but add a softer, more romantic aesthetic.

MINI ERASERS

Popular Japanese export items, erasers are usually sold in the form of pastries, ice cream, cartoon characters, or really any kind of design. You can generally find them in a craft store, while cabochons are usually specialty items found exclusively online. Attach them to your projects like you would cabochons or rhinestones, but be careful: They tend to be bulkier than other embellishments.

FOUND ITEMS

Pretty much anything that strikes your fancy can be attached to a DecoDen project. If you are a flea-market maven, old buttons, keys, and small toys work well as embellishments. If you love mosaic, small ceramic pieces or mirrors are great. For the beach combers, seashells and sea glass look lovely on trinket boxes, flower pots, and even cell-phone cases. Experiment! Finding the perfect embellishments is half the fun of DecoDen!

Make Your Own Cabochons

After your DecoDen obsession takes hold, buying cabochons can weigh heavily on your wallet. If you get really invested in the craft, you can undertake the fun and creative process of making your own custom cabochons. There are a few methods, all involving the use of silicone molds.

Silicone molds are often used in soap and chocolate making and are available in small sizes. You can also buy molds that are specifically made for cabochons.

Polymer clays like FIMO® and Sculpey® can be pressed into silicone molds for quick cabochons. Because the clay is precolored, using it will save you the step of painting your cabochons once they are complete. To use polymer clay, all you need to do is fill the mold, pop the clay out of the mold once the shape is set, and bake in an oven according to package instructions. If you are using multiple colors of clay in a single cabochon, simply fill the mold with a small amount of clay at a time and use a toothpick or other small tool to move the colors into place.

You can also use resin to make cabochons that you want to paint by hand, which will really allow you to include a bit of yourself into everything that you make. The most commonly used product for DecoDen is called EasyCast resin—because it is solvent free and low odor, it is ideal for indoor use. If you use resin to make cabochons, take note: Package instructions must be followed closely. Resin cabochons take around 72 hours to fully cure, so be sure to plan ahead.

Mod Melts are used with a high-heat glue gun to create your own cabochons. Squirt the melted liquid directly into a silicone mold, and in just 7 minutes the cabochon is dry. You can then remove the piece and paint as needed. **NOTE:** To give your cabochons a nice shine, paint them with a glossy decoupage glue when finished.

adhesives

WHIP

Special adhesives meant for DecoDen projects that looks like cake frosting when applied. Whip comes in a variety of icing-like colors (usually white, pink, brown, and mint green) and is sold in what looks and feels like icing piping bags. Different tips create different whip designs and motifs, but the most common tip is the star tip, which creates a traditional icing look.

WHITE SILICONE BATHROOM CAULK

When using silicone caulk, it's best to work in a well-ventilated room with open windows or even outside. Since you are working so intimately close to the caulk, wear a paper mask to avoid breathing in the harsh fumes and follow all of the label directions. You can either dispense the caulk into a piping bag or you can cut off the tip and securely tape on a star-shaped piping tip.

NOTE: If working with silicone, it is advisable to wear a mask.

DIMENSIONAL FABRIC PAINT

Dimensional paint comes in squeeze bottles with a fine tip and is traditionally used to decorate T-shirts and other fabric goods. In DecoDen it is used to create a delicious, drippy chocolate effect. Caramel colors and whites are other fantastic choices. While the paint is wet, press a rhinestone, flat-back pearl, or cabochon into the paint and let it dry for at least 24 hours (the paint is very thick, so drying takes time).

COLORED GLUE-GUN STICK

You will need a high-heat glue gun for this technique, but it is so worth it—the glue sticks allow you to get the same drippy effect as dimensional fabric paints, but in a much wider variety of colors. Just be careful to follow all package directions and do not to melt the surface to which you are gluing!

GLUE

Strong glue such as E6000® is perfect for attaching cabochons to your items when you don't want to use whip. It dries clear and creates a powerfully strong bond that will sustain a pretty significant impact. When working on small or narrow surfaces, use a toothpick to spread the glue around.

techniques

WHIP AND DRIZZLE

1. ZIGZAG
To make a zigzag design, use the star tip on the piping bag, holding the bag at an angle over the project. Squeeze the whip out while pulling the icing bag across your project. Gently press down as you move the bag across the project. This will form the first row. When you reach the end of the row, loop the bag in the opposite direction and apply a second row. Keep zigzagging back and forth until you reach the end. Press down at the end to seal.

2. STAR COVERED
Create a traditional star-covered design by using a star tip on a piping bag. Hold the bag upright about ¼ in. above the surface, squeeze the bag to release a star shape. Press gently on the surface and then quickly release the pressure as you pull the bag away.

3. SPOON SMEAR
Ice it like a cake with the back of a plastic spoon. Add a dollop of whip to the center and smooth the whip over the surface with the back of your spoon to achieve the perfect frosted effect!

4. DRIZZLED PAINT
Working on a piece of wax paper, balance the project on a block so that it's lifted from the work surface. Hold the dimensional fabric paint upright over the project and begin squeezing the paint as you move the bottle

quickly over the project to get the look of melted chocolate.

5. DRIPPY PAINT
Holding your project upright, apply dimensional fabric paint in a straight line where you want your drips to begin. With the paint bottle in one hand and the project in the other, go back over the painted line to add the drips by squeezing paint out onto the project at an angle. While you are painting move the project back and forth to move the paint. Dry flat for 24 hours before adding whip.

> **TIP** Although you can buy whip in a variety of colors, you can mix small amounts of paint into your whip yourself to achieve the perfect color for your projects! Always start out with just a little paint and add more as necessary. Make sure the whip is mixed well before using.

Sweet Paris Macaroon Phone Case

Everywhere we look, macaroon shops are popping up and tempting us with not only beautiful but delicious cookies. Their delicate colors and sweet style make them perfect for this cellphone case **(A)**. Make mini macaroons with molds or nab some from a DecoDen shop.

SKILL LEVEL

Beginner

MATERIALS

Cell phone cover

Whip of your choice

Piping bag

Star tip

Dimensional fabric paint of your choice

2 large Eiffel Tower embellishments

11 macaroon cookie embellishments

18 pastel colored rhinestones

Wax pencil

42 clear rhinestones, various sizes

Clear micro beads

Glue of your choice

VARIATION

Keep it monochromatic to make your cookies pop. Match your background and filler embellishments to the color of whip, like we did in the minty variation **(B)** to make your embellishments standout.

TO MAKE SWEET PARIS MACAROON PHONE CASE

1. Using a star tip, apply the whip in a star fashion to the top of the case. Drizzle the dimensional paint over the case in a crisscross fashion.

2. Embed the 2 Eiffel Towers into the whip near the center. Press to secure. Add the cookies around the Eiffel Towers in a random pattern and at different angles.

3. Using a wax pencil, fill in the design with colored and clear rhinestones. Sprinkle micro beads over the entire design.

4. Glue small rhinestones to any empty spots on the design. Allow to dry for 24 to 72 hours before use.

Bakery Cakes Phone Case

Tiny cakes are the star attraction on this phone case. Load them up at different angles to show off all their miniature details.

SKILL LEVEL
Beginner

MATERIALS
Cell phone cover
Whip of your choice
Piping bag
Star tip
Glitter
20 mini cake embellishments
Wax pencil
30 purple heart rhinestones
20 purple pearls
20 clear rhinestones

TO MAKE BAKERY CAKES PHONE CASE

1. Using a star tip, apply the whip in a star fashion to the top of the case. Sprinkle the top with glitter.

2. Begin to embed the cakes by pressing into the whip. Embed them at different angles and directions.

3. Using a wax pencil, fill in the design with the hearts, pearls, and rhinestones. Allow to dry for 24 to 72 hours before use.

TIP Design it! When working with various colors and shapes of embellishments, it's a good idea to lay out a design plan before you begin to embed. Remember your design plan with a photo or quick sketch.

No-Bake Cake Slices

Kitchen sponges get a sweet makeover with the help of a little whip and lots of imagination. Added bonus: There are no calories in this vanilla cake **(A)**!

SKILL LEVEL
Beginner

MATERIALS
Yellow kitchen sponges, 2 per slice
Scissors
Whip of your choice
Piping bag
Large star tip
Glitter

TO MAKE NO-BAKE CAKE SLICES

1. Cut the sponges into cake slice shapes.

2. Pipe pink whip on the top of one of the sponges. Place the other sponge on top of the whip and press to secure. Pipe a decorative border where the two sponges meet.

3. Using the star tip, pipe white whip stars on the top of the top sponge. Sprinkle glitter over the design. Allow the whip to harden for a few hours.

4. Pipe large elongated stars along the backside of the cake and to the top border edge. Allow to dry for 24 to 72 hours before use.

VARIATION
The chocolate variation **(B)** features a drizzle and pearl design. To make the whip smooth like frosting, just pipe a little brown tinted whip onto the sponge cake and smooth with the back of a plastic spoon. Pipe decorative stars along the border edge in pink and white whip. Allow to harden for 2 hours. Tape off the sides of the cake with low-tack painters' tape to protect the sides. Drizzle dimensional fabric paint over the top. Once dry, glue small heart pearls to the top.

Posh Parfait Treats

Fool your friends with these deco ice cream treats! Make big ones for displaying in your home **(A)** or make mini ones for an afternoon of make-believe around a child's tea table **(B)**.

TO MAKE POSH PARFAIT TREATS

1. Drizzle the chocolate brown dimensional paint around the inside of the parfait cup and allow to fully dry, between 2 and 4 hours.

2. Using a foam paintbrush, paint the inside of the parfait cup and the Styrofoam ball with a pastel color of whip. Add a dollop of whip in the bottom of the cup and place the ball into the dollop. Press to secure. Add more whip to the top to fill the cup if needed. Allow to harden for 2 hours.

3. Using the star tip, pipe white whip stars on the top of the parfait so that it looks like whipped cream. Drizzle clear glitter dimensional paint over the white whip.

4. Embed the straws and cookies into the white whip. Add the sprinkles around the whipped design.

5. Using the star tip, add elongated stars in pink whip around the outer edge of the parfait cup. Allow to dry for 24 to 48 hours, depending on how much whip you use.

TIP Shop supplies! Look for mini parfait cups in the wedding section of your local craft store. They usually come in sets of 12, making them a great craft for slumber parties.

Palm Beach Phone Case

Show off your party-girl style with a neon flower cell phone case. This would be the perfect accessory for hanging poolside in the sun.

TIP Color cues! If you are stumped for a color plan, let the object you are decorating do the work. For this cell phone case, we matched the flowers to the hot pink color of the case.

SKILL LEVEL

Beginner

MATERIALS

Cell phone cover

Whip of your choice

Piping bag

Star tip

Glitter

3 large pink flowers

7 medium piña colada embellishments

3 large turquoise heart rhinestones

5 medium silver gumdrop rhinestones

5 medium flower rhinestones

Wax pencil

12 small turquoise rhinestones

10 small clear rhinestones

TO MAKE PALM BEACH PHONE CASE

1. Using a star tip, apply the whip in a star fashion to the top of the cell phone case. Sprinkle the top with glitter.

2. Begin by embedding the 3 large flowers. Scatter them so they fill the phone case.

3. Group the piña colada embellishments into small clusters around each flower. Embed a turquoise heart around each grouping.

4. Add the gumdrop and flower rhinestones to the design. Using a wax pencil, embed the small rhinestones all around the design.

Donut Shop Tablet Cover

Heads will turn when you whip out this blinged-out sugary tablet case. Keep it themed by using a small color pallet and use donuts of various sizes for extra interest.

SKILL LEVEL

Intermediate

MATERIALS

Tablet cover

Dimensional fabric paint, chocolate brown

Whip of your choice, tinted brown

Piping bag

Star tip

Plastic spoon

Brown glitter

8 large donuts

23 small donuts

Wax pencil

36 peach heart pearls

40 pink pearls

20 small blue rhinestones

TO MAKE DONUT SHOP TABLET COVER

1. Drizzle dimensional paint across three-fourths of the case at an angle. Allow to dry for 24 hours before applying the whip.

2. Using a star tip, apply the whip to the tablet case. Use the back of a plastic spoon to smear the whip flat. Sprinkle the top with glitter.

3. Begin by embedding the large donuts across the case. Next, add the small donuts.

4. Using a wax pencil, apply the hearts, pearls, and rhinestones to the whip. Allow to dry for 24 to 72 hours.

> TIP Keep it drippy! When using whip over drippy dimensional paint, make sure you overlap a little bit of the whip onto the edge of the drippy paint.

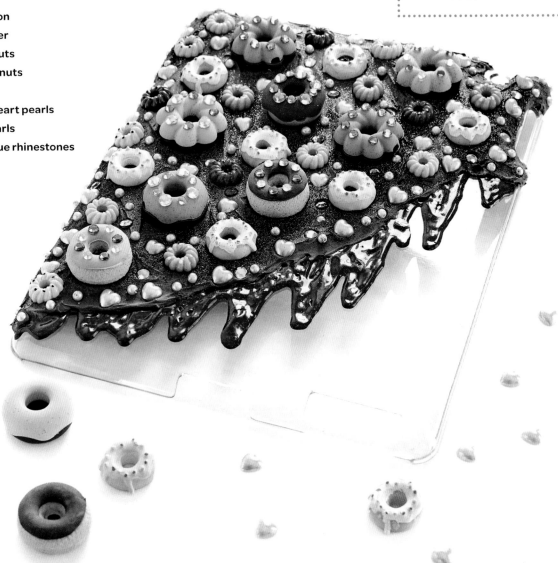

Bakery Bling Three-Tiered Cake

Girls of all ages will love a blinged-out cake. Pearls, rhinestones, and miniature flowers are the perfect embellishments for an over-the-top design.

SKILL LEVEL
Intermediate

MATERIALS

Two 8-in. Styrofoam round disks
Two 6-in. Styrofoam round disks
Two 4-in. Styrofoam round disks
Glue of your choice
Heart-shaped piece of wood
Whip of your choice
Piping bag
Star piping tip
Glitter
8 purple mini silk flowers
25 large purple rhinestones
150 purple pearls, various sizes
8 blue mini silk flowers
16 large blue rhinestones
120 blue pearls, various sizes
8 pink mini silk flowers
16 large pink rhinestones
100 pink pearls, various sizes
17 clear heart rhinestones
30 white pearls, various sizes

TO MAKE BAKERY BLING THREE-TIERED CAKE

1. Glue the 8-in. disks together, the 6-in. disks together, and the 4-in. disks together. Glue the disks to form a cake shape with the 8-in. disks on the bottom, the 6-in. disks in the middle and the 4-in. disks on the top. Press the heart-shaped wood into the center of the top tier.

2. Using a star tip, apply whip over the entire cake shape and the heart. Sprinkle glitter over the entire cake and heart.

3. Embed each layer with a different color of embellishments. Press the embellishments into the whip firmly. Use the purple rhinestones, pearls, and flowers on the bottom layer. Use the blue embellishments on the center layer and the pink embellishments on the top layer.

4. Decorate the heart with clear heart rhinestones and white pearls. Allow to dry for 24 to 72 hours.

> **TIP** Go ombré! Make it ombré by using one color in three different shades. Use the darker shade on the bottom tier, the medium shade on the middle tier and the lightest shade on the top tier.

Lemon and Lime Treats

Not everything sweet is chocolate. These lemon **(A)** and lime treats **(B)** use mini pie tart pans and silicon cupcake liners as the perfect vessels for whip.

SKILL LEVEL
Beginner

MATERIALS
Whip of your choice

Tan acrylic craft paint

Mini pie tart pan

Plastic knife

Yellow acrylic craft paint

Piping bag

Star tip

Yellow glitter

2 green sparkle beads

TO MAKE LEMON AND LIME TREATS

1. Mix a small amount of tan paint with white whip until you have the color of pie crust. Apply the pie crust color–whip to the inside edges of the tart pan with a plastic knife. Allow to harden for 2 hours.

2. Make yellow whip and fill the piping bag. Using a star tip, apply the whip to the inside of the pan in a spiral fashion. Sprinkle yellow glitter over the design.

3. Using the star tip, pipe mini stars along the edge where the yellow whip meets the crust.

4. Press 2 beads into the center of the tart. Allow to dry for 24 hours.

17

Ice Cream Business Card Cases

If you have a sweet idea for a business then this is the case for you! Load it up with ice creams of various sizes and make a chilled-out ice-blue whip for the base **(A)**.

SKILL LEVEL
Beginner

MATERIALS

Business card case

Whip of your choice, tinted blue

Piping bag

Star tip

Blue glitter

1 large ice cream cone embellishments

16 small ice cream cone embellishments

Wax pencil

10 blue flower embellishments

12 yellow star embellishments

12 pink star embellishments

12 pink rhinestones

TO MAKE ICE CREAM BUSINESS CARD CASES

1. Using a star tip, apply the whip to the card case. Sprinkle the top with glitter.

2. Begin by embedding the large ice cream cone in the center of the case. Next, add the remaining ice cream cones around the large one.

3. Using a wax pencil, apply the flowers, stars, and rhinestones to the design. Allow to dry for 24 hours.

VARIATION

Show off your sweet side. Make a desktop design **(B)** by gluing ice cream–themed embellishments and rhinestones to a clear business card stand.

Sweet Treat Lanyards

Flash some candy next time you have to show your ID. It's as easy as pie to make these lanyards: All you need is a little glue and some sweet embellishments.

SKILL LEVEL
Beginner

MATERIALS
ID lanyard
Glue of your choice
Toothpick
Candy embellishments
Rhinestones
Wax pencil

TO MAKE SWEET TREAT LANYARDS

1. Layout a design plan with your embellishments.

2. Apply glue to the back of each embellishment with a toothpick and apply around the outer edge of the lanyard case.

3. Using glue and a wax pencil, attach rhinestones to the design. Allow to dry 4 to 8 hours.

TIP Get level! When gluing to an item that is not flat on the back, try placing the item in a bowl of dried beans. You can move the item and beans around until the item is level.

Time for Fruit Tarts Clock

What time is it? It's time to brighten up a kitchen nook with this fruit tart–inspired clock. For this design we used a combination of erasers, mini cakes, and fruit embellishments, but you can theme yours around any favorite snack!

SKILL LEVEL
Beginner

MATERIALS
Clock with a wide rim
Glue of your choice
Toothpick
7 large tart embellishments
14 small tart and cake embellishments
15 cherry embellishments
12 strawberry embellishments
Wax pencil
55 small green rhinestones

TO MAKE TIME FOR FRUIT TARTS CLOCK

1. Layout a design plan with your embellishments.

2. Apply glue to the back of each embellishment with a toothpick. Apply each embellishment around the rim of the clock.

3. Using glue and a wax pencil, attach rhinestones to the design. Allow to dry for at least 24 hours before hanging.

TIP Make clusters! If you are layering embellishments, try gluing them into clusters before you glue them to your project.

Sweet Shoppe Monogram

Customize your room by creating a candy-coated monogram. Apply decorative paper to the letter first and then layer on the sweet stuff.

SKILL LEVEL
Intermediate

MATERIALS
Wooden letter
Sweets-themed scrapbook paper
Foam paintbrush
Decoupage glue of your choice
Decorative trim
Whip of your choice, tinted pink
Piping bag
Star tip
Glitter
Dimensional fabric paint, purple
9 wafer heart embellishments
7 cake embellishments
3 chocolate bar embellishments
7 large heart rhinestones
Wax pencil
27 medium purple rhinestones
12 mini mint green pearls

TO MAKE SWEET SHOP MONOGRAM

1. Trim the paper to fit the front of the letter. Apply decoupage glue to the back of the paper with the foam brush. Position the paper onto the letter. Smooth with your fingers to press out any air bubbles. Top-coat the letter with a thin layer of decoupage glue and allow to dry.

2. Glue trim around the outer edge of the letter.

3. Apply whip to the lower portion of the letter using a star tip. Sprinkle glitter over the design. Drizzle paint over the whip.

4. Embed the wafer hearts, cakes, chocolate bars, and the large heart rhinestones into the whip. Using a wax pencil, embed some of the medium rhinestones and pearls to the design.

5. Glue the rest of the medium rhinestones to the paper portion of the letter. Allow to dry at least 24 hours before hanging.

> **TIP** Add paper! When working on a large design use printed papers or fabrics to fill in areas on the project. Decorative paper can be found for 25¢ a sheet at craft and hobby stores.

Cute as a Cupcake Vanity Set

Add a bit of sugar and spice to your morning routine with this cupcake-inspired vanity set.

SKILL LEVEL
Beginner

MATERIALS

Plastic vanity set

Whip of your choice, tinted to match vanity set

Piping bag

Star tip

Glitter

2 large cupcake embellishments

4 small cupcake embellishments

4 bow embellishments

9 brown pearls

Wax pencil

23 clear rhinestones

TO MAKE CUTE AS A CUPCAKE VANITY SET

1. Using a star tip, apply the whip to the fronts of the vanity set. Sprinkle with glitter.

2. Embed the large cupcakes in the center by pressing into the whip. Add the smaller cupcakes and bows to the sides of the center design.

3. Press the pearls into the whip. Using a wax pencil, attach the small rhinestones to the design. Allow to dry 24 to 48 hours.

TIP Dollar store it! Look for objects to DecoDen at your local dollar store or thrift shop. This vanity set was under 2 bucks and is a perfect canvas for whip!

Looking Yummy Hand Mirror

Mirror, mirror in my hand, who is the sweetest in the land? Why this delicious mirror is!

SKILL LEVEL
Beginner

MATERIALS
Hand mirror

Whip of your choice, tinted hot pink

Piping bag

Mini star tip

Dimensional fabric paint, white

1 large ice cream embellishment

Gold letters (to spell *yummy* or any other word)

Glue of your choice

7 large black heart embellishments

6 pink heart rhinestones

2 pearl hearts

10 small heart rhinestones

9 pink pearls

4 pink gumdrop beads

4 gold mini fans

2 mini pearl hearts

Micro beads, gold

TO MAKE LOOKING YUMMY HAND MIRROR

1. Using a mini star tip, apply the whip to the back of the hand mirror. Drizzle with white pearl paint.

2. Embed the large ice cream embellishment in the center by pressing into the whip. Add the letters across the top of the mirror.

3. Glue 2 black hearts and 1 pink heart to the handle of the mirror.

4. Embed the pearl hearts, rhinestone hearts, pearls, gumdrop beads, mini fans, mini pearl hearts, and the rest of the black and pink hearts into the whip.

5. Sprinkle the gold beads over the design. Allow to dry for 24 to 48 hours and tap off any excess rhinestones.

> **TIP** Mix it up! Combine whip embedded embellishments with glued embellishments to create a layered design.

VARIATIONS

Adorably sweet! Make a necklace with just a hint of sweet by gluing two ice cream cones to a statement necklace **(B)**.

Charmingly sweet! Make a maxi charm necklace by gluing sweet embellishments to small bails and then attaching them to a chain **(C)**.

Pop Love Necklace

Large ice-pop erasers and mini star rhinestones are the perfect embellishments for this pop-star-inspired necklace **(A)**.

SKILL LEVEL
Beginner

MATERIALS
Acrylic or plastic statement pendant
Whip of your choice
Piping bag
Star tip
Neon pink glitter
2 large ice-pop embellishments
Wax pencil
1 pink bow embellishment
6 pearl hearts
10 pink star embellishments
12 yellow star embellishments
15 mini rhinestones

TO MAKE POP LOVE NECKLACE

1. Using a star tip, apply the whip to the pendant. Sprinkle with glitter.

2. Embed the ice pops into the center of the pendant by pressing into the whip.

3. Using a wax pencil, fill in the design with the bow, hearts, stars, and rhinestones. Allow to dry for 4 to 8 hours.

Ice Cream Bling Bracelets

Ice cream embellishments and a little glue are all you need to alter store-bought bracelets **(A)** into DecoDen bling jewelry.

SKILL LEVEL

Beginner

MATERIALS

Bracelet
Glue of your choice
Toothpick
Ice cream embellishments
Wax pencil
Rhinestones

TO MAKE ICE CREAM BLING BRACELETS

1. Using a toothpick, apply glue to the back of the ice cream embellishments and attach to the bracelet.

2. Using the wax pencil and glue, attach rhinestones to the bracelet.

VARIATION

Glue your sweets onto a watch or watchstrap **(B)** for another great fashion statement. Just make sure you glue everything on so that it is centered when the strap is clasped around your wrist!

Deco the Halls Holiday Gift Tin

Layer up holiday sweets like gingerbread people, candy canes, and peppermints on the top of a gift tin for a truly fun way to wrap any present.

SKILL LEVEL
Beginner

MATERIALS
Small gift tin
Whip of your choice
Piping bag
Star tip
Glitter

Dimensional fabric paint, silver glitter
6 large gingerbread people embellishments
7 candy cane embellishments
5 small gingerbread people embellishments
7 snowflake embellishments
5 wrapped candy embellishments
11 small peppermint candy embellishments
4 pearl hearts
15 rhinestones

TO MAKE DECO THE HALLS HOLIDAY GIFT TIN

1. Using a star tip, apply the whip to top of the tin lid. Sprinkle with glitter. Drizzle silver paint over the design.

2. Embed the large gingerbread people by pressing into the whip. Embed the candy canes around the edge of the tin. Fill in the design with small gingerbread people, snowflakes, wrapped candy, and small peppermint candies.

3. Press the pearl hearts and rhinestones into the design.

TIP Holiday hoarding! Gather supplies for holiday DecoDen designs during the holidays from your local craft store or home store. Small ornaments and scrapbooking embellishments are perfect for embedding and gluing onto any project.

TIP Recycled rack! Fashion a ring drying rack by turning a closed egg carton upside down, cut slits into the bottom of the egg holder and place the ring into the slit.

Sugar and Spice Rings

Mini desserts take center stage on a simple ring base.

SKILL LEVEL

Beginner

MATERIALS

Ring base

Glue of your choice

Toothpick

Dessert embellishments

Bowl of dried beans

Wax pencil

Gem glue

Rhinestones

**TO MAKE SUGAR
AND SPICE RINGS**

1. Using a toothpick, apply glue to the back of the embellishments and attach them to the ring base. Balance the ring in a bowl of dried beans while drying.

2. Optional, using the wax pencil and gem glue, attach rhinestones around the dessert embellishment.

TIP Stuff it! Stuff soft projects with recycled paper to add support while whipping, gluing, and drying.

VARIATION

Go glam by losing the whip and applying rhinestones **(B)**. Glue just a few chocolates to the top of the sneaker and then glue rhinestones to the canvas. Hide glue marks when gluing rhinestones to canvas by glittering the canvas first with a flat paintbrush and glitter glue. The glitter will disguise any glue marks.

Chocoholic Sneakers

Show off your love for chocolate with each step in these chocolate-encrusted sneakers **(A)**. Whether you're coming or going, everyone will be sure to notice if you're wearing these!

SKILL LEVEL

Intermediate

MATERIALS

Canvas sneakers

Whip of your choice

Piping bag

Star tip

Glitter

Pearl trim

40 chocolate embellishments

50 green pearls

90 brown pearls

30 white pearls

Wax pencil

60 small green rhinestones

TO MAKE CHOCOHOLIC SNEAKERS

1. Using a star tip, apply the whip to the tops and back heel of the sneakers. Sprinkle with glitter. Press the pearl trim around the top edge of the whip.

2. Separate the embellishments into two piles (one for each sneaker). Embed the chocolate sweets onto the shoes by pressing into the whip.

3. Press the pearls into the whip. Using a wax pencil, attach small rhinestones to the design. Allow to dry for 48 to 72 hours.

Birthday Treats Frame

Create a handmade DecoDen birthday frame for your favorite sweetie! Make the cakes using a mold and customize the color with any paint you choose.

SKILL LEVEL

Beginner

MATERIALS

Wood heart frame

Whip of your choice

Piping bag

Star tip

Yellow glitter

2 large cake embellishments

Happy birthday banner embellishment

8 ice cream scoop embellishments

2 lollipop embellishments

9 chocolate bar embellishments

4 wafer cookie embellishments

6 large pink rhinestones

14 brown pearls

6 pink pearls

18 green small pearls

Wax pencil

65 small rhinestones

TO MAKE BIRTHDAY TREATS FRAME

1. Using a star tip, apply the whip to top of the frame. Border the heart edge with a decorative whipped edge. Sprinkle with glitter.

2. Embed the large cake embellishments near the sides of the heart by pressing into the whip. Add the banner to the top and bottom of the frame. Add the ice cream and lollypop embellishments. Fill in the design with the small chocolate bars and cookies.

3. Press the large pink rhinestones and the pearls into the whip. Using a wax pencil, attach small rhinestones to the design. Allow to dry for 24 to 48 hours.

> **TIP** Customize it! Add number embellishments or personalized name banners to the frame to create a one-of-a-kind DecoDen project.

resources

MICHAELS® STORES

www.Michaels.com

Silicone molds

EasyCast resin

Mod Podge® Collage Clay

Mod Podge Mod Melts and Molds

Fine glitters

Embellishments, such as rhinestones, beads, and charms

Dimensional fabric paint

Polymer clay

SOPHIE & TOFFEE

sophieandtoffee.com

DecoDen supplies

ETSY™

www.etsy.com

DecoDen supplies

Cabochons

AMAZON®

www.amazon.com

DecoDen supplies

Cabochons

eBAY®

www.ebay.com

Cabochons

Molds

Modeling clay

Tools

Findings

DecoDen whip

DELISH BEADS

www.delishbeads.com

Beads

Cabochons

Findings

ROCKIN' RESIN

www.rockinresin.com

Cabochons

IT'S CUTE

www.decoden-acc.com

DecoDen supplies

If you like these projects, you'll love these other fun craft booklets

DecoDen Bling
Mini decorations for phones & favorite things

Alice Fisher

DecoDen is all about bringing bling to every aspect of your life—from your sunglasses to your cellphone to everything in between! Best of all, the decadent sparkle of this hot decorating technique is just a few simple techniques away. From phone cases to wall clocks to picture frames and more, the 20 recipes in this booklet will show you exactly what you need to glam up your day.

32 pages, product #078046, $9.95 U.S.

Bungee Band Bracelets & More
12 projects to make with bungee band & paracord

Vera Vandenbosch

Bungee cord is no longer just a tool—now available in a wide variety of colors and thicknesses, it's the perfect material for you to create beautiful bracelets and necklaces. The 12 projects in this booklet will show you exactly how to transform this stretchy material into runway-worthy designs for you to wear and show off.

32 pages, product #078048, $9.95 U.S.

Arm Knitting
chunky cowls, scarves, and other no-needle knits

Linda Zemba Burhance

Knitting your own scarf, cowl, or blanket is easier than you think, and with the brilliant new technique called arm knitting, it couldn't be quicker. Each of these 12 projects knit up in under an hour and only require a few skeins of yarn. Best of all, you don't need any tools—just bring your arms and hands! Go wild with the bright colors of the Fun Times Scarf, add a sophisticated layer to your date night outfit with the Evening Sparkle Tie-on Shrug, or just cuddle up with the Super Cozy Throw. Just know that your friends are going to want some of their own!

32 pages, product #078045, $9.95 U.S.

Shop for these and other great craft books and booklets online: www.tauntonstore.com

Simply search by product number or call 800-888-8286, use code MX800126

Call Monday-Friday 9AM - 9PM EST and Saturday 9AM - 5PM EST • International customers, call 203-702-2204

Look for these other *Threads* Selects booklets at www.tauntonstore.com and wherever crafts are sold.

Button Jewelry
Susan Beal

EAN: 9781627107808
8½ x 10⅞, 32 pages
Product# 078040
$9.95 U.S., $9.95 Can.

Bead Necklaces
Susan Beal

EAN: 9781621137641
8½ x 10⅞, 32 pages
Product# 078002
$9.95 U.S., $9.95 Can.

Drop Earrings
Susan Beal

EAN: 9781621137658
8½ x 10⅞, 32 pages
Product# 078003
$9.95 U.S., $9.95 Can.

Bead Bracelets
Susan Beal

EAN: 9781621139515
8½ x 10⅞, 32 pages
Product # 078028
$9.95 U.S., $9.95 Can.

Crocheted Hearts & Flowers
Vanessa Mooncie

EAN: 9781627107761
8½ x 10⅞, 32 pages
Product# 078044
$9.95 U.S., $9.95 Can.

Prairie Girl Gifts
Jennifer Worick

EAN: 9781621139492
8½ x 10⅞, 32 pages
Product # 078030
$9.95 U.S., $9.95 Can.

DIY Bride: Cakes & Sweets
Khris Cochran

EAN: 9781621137665
8½ x 10⅞, 32 pages
Product# 078004
$9.95 U.S., $9.95 Can.

DIY Bride: Beautiful Bouquets
Khris Cochran

EAN: 9781621137672
8½ x 10⅞, 32 pages
Product# 078005
$9.95 U.S., $9.95 Can.

DIY Bride: Perfect Invitations
Khris Cochran

EAN: 9781621139522
8½ x 10⅞, 32 pages
Product # 078027
$9.95 U.S., $9.95 Can.

Great Cupcakes

EAN: 9781627107778
8½ x 10⅞, 32 pages
Product # 078041
$9.95 U.S., $9.95 Can.

Easy-to-Sew Flowers

EAN: 9781621138259
8½ x 10⅞, 32 pages
Product # 078017
$9.95 U.S., $9.95 Can.

Beaded Gifts

EAN: 9781627107730
8½ x 10⅞, 32 pages
Product# 078039
$9.95 U.S., $9.95 Can.